This book belongs to _K Jeran_

Age _9_

Favourite player _Jakavic Adams_

Prediction of Blues' final position this season _9th_

Prediction of Championship winners this season

newcastel

Prediction of FA Cup winners this season

chealsc

Prediction of EFL Cup winners this season

Manchester united

Prediction of teams to be relegated
from the Championship this season:

22nd _____

23rd _Villa_

24th _____

Written by twocan

Contributors:
Colin Tattum & Rob Mason

A TWOCAN PUBLICATION

©2016. Published by twocan under licence from Birmingham City FC.

Every effort has been made to ensure the accuracy of information within this publication but the publishers cannot be held responsible for any errors or omissions.

Views expressed are those of the author and do not necessarily represent those of the publishers or the football club.

ISBN 978-1-909872-80-6

PICTURE CREDITS
Press Association
Action Images

£8

CONTENTS

2016/17

Back row (from left): Phil Sanders (Bootroom Assistant), Andy Johnson (Strength and Conditioning Coach Professional), Dan Millard (Assistant Tactical Analyst), Charlee Adams, Josh Cogley, Ryan Shotton, Darren Robinson (Head of Recruitment), Clayton Donaldson, Viv Solomon-Otabor, Jack Storer, Jon Seeley (Masseur), Tom Page (Sports Scientist Professional), Paul Doherty (Masseur).

Middle row (from left): Dave Hunt (First Team Physiotherapist), Pete Shaw (Head Physiotherapist), Jonathan Grounds, Koby Arthur, Stephen Gleeson, David Cotterill, Adam Legzdins, Tomasz Kuszczak, Connal Trueman, Reece Brown, Andrew Shinnie, James Vaughan, David Davis, David James (Assistant Kit Manager), Jon Pearce (Kit Manager).

Front row (from left): Kevin Poole (Goalkeeping Coach), Dave Carolan (Head of Sports Science), Robert Tesche, Paul Caddis, Jonathan Spector, Michael Morrison, Kevin Summerfield (Assistant Manager), Gary Rowett (Manager), Mark Sale (First Team Coach), Paul Robinson, Diego Fabbrini, Jacques Maghoma, Maikel Kieftenbeld, Richard Beale (Senior Professional Development Coach), Joe Carnall (Head of Tactical Analysis).

Jonathan 29Y
GROUNDS | 03

Position: Defender **Nationality:** English **DOB:** 02.02.88

Grounds joined Blues in the summer of 2014 and firmly established himself as a regular in the first team. He operates predominantly as a left-back but can also stand in at centre-back if required.

Adam 30Y
LEGZDINS | 01

Position: Goalkeeper **Nationality:** English **DOB:** 28.11.86

Legzdins rejoined Blues for a second time last summer. He made his debut in the 2-1 League Cup win at Bristol Rovers in August 2015 and during the 2015/16 campaign went on to make a further seven appearances.

Paul
ROBINSON | 04

Position: Defender **Nationality:** English **DOB:** 17.12.78

An experienced defender, Robinson signed a new one-year contract in May 2016. He will take on a player-coach role at St Andrew's, where he will also help develop Gary Rowett's U21s and U18s.

Maikel
KIEFTENBELD | 06

Position: Midfielder **Nationality:** Dutch **DOB:** 26.06.90

Kieftenbeld joined Blues in July 2015 from FC Groningen. He made a total of 46 appearances during his first season with Birmingham and found the back of the net three times. He has been capped five times for his country at U21 level.

Ryan
SHOTTON | 05

Position: Defender **Nationality:** English **DOB:** 30.09.88

Shotton joined Blues this summer following a successful loan spell in early 2016. Last season he made two appearances at right-back, before partnering Morrison in the heart of defence for the final six games.

SQUAD 2016/17

Robert
TESCHE
07

Position: Midfielder **Nationality:** German **DOB:** 27.05.87

Blues completed the signing of Tesche in June 2016 after a previous successful loan spell at the end of the 2014/15 season. A skilful, ball-playing midfielder, he is able to dictate the play and is adept at shooting from distance.

Stephen
GLEESON
08

Position: Midfielder **Nationality:** Irish **DOB:** 03.08.88

A former MK Dons midfielder and Republic of Ireland international, Gleeson joined Birmingham City in June 2014 and has since established himself as a first team regular. He hit the net five times last season.

Clayton
DONALDSON
09

Position: Striker **Nationality:** Jamaican **DOB:** 07.02.84

Blues signed Donaldson in the summer of 2014. In his debut season he was awarded both Players' Player and Supporters' Player of the Season awards and 2015/16 saw him top Blues' scoring charts with an 11-goal tally.

David COTTERILL | 11

Position: Midfielder **Nationality:** Welsh **DOB:** 04.12.87

Cardiff-born Cotterill made the switch to Blues ahead of the 2014/15 campaign and has been a regular feature for the past two seasons. He can play on either flank and is also a Wales international.

Diego FABBRINI | 10

Position: Striker **Nationality:** Italian **DOB:** 31.07.90

Blues completed the permanent signing of Fabbrini from Watford in January 2016. He can play in a variety of positions across the front line and returned to Blues following a successful loan spell in 2014/15.

Rhoys WIGGINS | 12

Position: Defender **Nationality:** Welsh **DOB:** 04.11.87

Wiggins joined Blues on loan on the final day of the summer 2016 transfer window. He is a former Wales U21 international and was called up to the senior squad for Euro 2016 qualifying matches although didn't get any game time.

Lukas JUTKIEWICZ | 15

Position: Striker **Nationality:** English **DOB:** 28.03.89

Jutkiewicz joined Blues on loan from Burnley on 31 August 2016, with the loan period running until 2 January 2017. He brings a wealth of experience to the side, having spent time at number of different clubs.

Che ADAMS | 14

Position: Striker **Nationality:** English **DOB:** 13.07.96

A former England U20 international, Adams moved to Blues this summer from Sheffield United. He penned a three-year deal at St Andrew's and can operate as an attacking midfielder or striker.

Charlee ADAMS | 16

Position: Midfielder **Nationality:** English **DOB:** 16.02.95

Adams joined Blues as a scholar in the summer of 2011 after leaving the West Ham Academy. Last season he made his first start for the first team in the final game of the campaign away at Cardiff City.

Jacques MAGHOMA | 19

Position: Midfielder **Nationality:** Congolese **DOB:** 23.10.87

Maghoma joined Blues in June 2015 and during a successful first season, he made a total of 44 appearances and scored six goals. He has also earned several full international caps with DR Congo.

Viv SOLOMON-OTABOR | 17

Position: Midfielder **Nationality:** English **DOB:** 02.01.96

A quick and powerful winger, Solomon-Otabor signed his first professional deal in June 2014. He scored his first senior goal with a fantastic solo effort, in the 5-2 thrashing of Fulham in November 2015.

Reece BROWN | 18

Position: Midfielder **Nationality:** English **DOB:** 03.03.96

Brown has been with the club since the age of ten and made rapid progress through the Academy ranks. In June 2016, he signed a one-year contract extension with Blues which will run until 2017.

Greg
STEWART
20

Position: Striker Nationality: Scottish DOB: 17.03.90

Stewart joined Blues from Scottish Premier League side Dundee in August 2016 on a three-year deal. A former Rangers and Hearts academy product, he can play in any of the front four positions.

Andrew
SHINNIE
22

Position: Midfielder Nationality: Scottish DOB: 17.07.89

Shinnie joined Blues in 2013 after his contract with Inverness Caledonian Thistle came to an end. He took in a loan spell at Rotherham United last season, where he made a total of three appearances for the Millers.

Jonathan SPECTOR | 23

Position: Defender **Nationality:** American **DOB:** 01.03.86

An American international, Spector joined Blues at the start of August 2011. He is a versatile player who can play in both midfield and across defence. He signed a new two-year deal with Birmingham last summer.

Koby ARTHUR | 24

Position: Midfielder **Nationality:** Ghanaian **DOB:** 31.01.96

A highly-rated young midfielder, Arthur is a powerful striker of the ball and can play anywhere across the middle of the park or in a more advanced role. He signed a new two-year deal with Blues in June 2015.

Josh COGLEY | 25

Position: Defender **Nationality:** English **DOB:** 12.03.96

A product of the Club's Academy, Cogley joined Blues back in 2011. He has been a regular with the U21 side and was issued a first team squad number this summer as a result of his impressive performances during pre-season.

David
DAVIS

28

Position: Midfielder **Nationality:** English **DOB:** 20.02.91

A powerful midfielder, Davis joined Blues in August 2014 from Wolves. During his six-year spell at Molineux, he also spent time out on loan with Walsall, Shrewsbury Town, Inverness Caledonian Thistle and Chesterfield.

Connal
TRUEMAN

27

Position: Goalkeeper **Nationality:** English **DOB:** 26.03.96

Trueman was handed a first team squad number ahead of Blues' Championship away fixture at Blackburn Rovers in October 2014. He was on the subs' bench for the game but has yet to make a first team appearance.

Michael
MORRISON

28

Position: Defender **Nationality:** English **DOB:** 03.03.88

Morrison signed a permanent deal with Blues in January 2015 and has firmly established himself as a first team regular. He plays predominantly as a centre-half, but can also slot in at full-back if required.

Tomasz
KUSZCZAK

29

Position: Goalkeeper **Nationality:** Polish **DOB:** 20.03.82

A former Polish international goalkeeper, Kuszczak joined Blues last summer on a two-year deal after leaving Wolves. His first season at St Andrew's saw him make 42 appearances.

Jack STORER

38

Position: Striker **Nationality:** English **DOB:** 02.01.98

Previously a member of Blues' Academy, Storer was re-signed as an addition to the Development Squad this summer. But his impressive form during pre-season, scoring seven goals in seven appearances, saw him elevated to the senior squad.

Paul CADDIS

31

Position: Defender **Nationality:** Scottish **DOB:** 19.04.88

Caddis joined Blues from Swindon Town back in August 2013 and has been a regular ever since. A former Scotland U21 international, he plays predominantly at right-back, but has also featured occasionally in midfield.

Nicolai BROCK-MADSEN

44

Position: Striker **Nationality:** Danish **DOB:** 09.01.93

A former Danish U21 striker, Brock-Madsen joined Blues from Danish Superliga club Randers FC in August 2015. He made his Blues debut the same month as a substitute in the capital Cup second round victory against Gillingham.

03 Jonathan Grounds

A

Birmingham were promoted this season after finishing second in Division 2

Can you work out in which season each of these photos was taken?

There's a clue to help you with each one!

B

Blues won promotion to the First Division this season after finishing third in the table

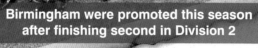

C

This was the first season Blues played under the name 'Birmingham', having previously played as 'Small Heath'

D

Captain Paul Robinson signed for Birmingham this season

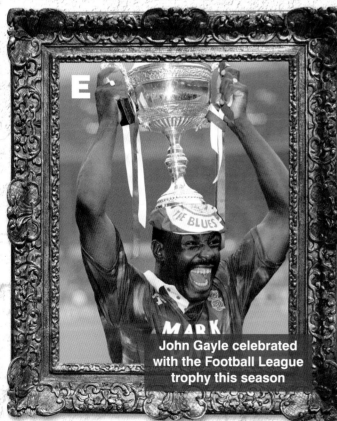

E

John Gayle celebrated with the Football League trophy this season

spot the

Season

Here is the first half of our Championship A-Z. The answer to each clue begins with the corresponding letter of the alphabet.

A-Z OF THE

A Newcastle were relegated to the Championship last season after finishing 18th, but this club was bottom of the table

B The creatures present on Brentford's club crest

C Manager of Burton Albion when they were promoted from League One last season

D Preston North End play their home games here

E Wolves midfielder who was in Wales' squad for Euro 2016

F Name of Brighton's stadium before it was sponsored by AMEX

G Reading's top appearance maker last season

CHAMPIONSHIP

I Derby play their home games here

H Blackburn's player of the 2015/16 season

Leeds United's kit manufacturer

J Wigan's Finnish goalie who helped them reach promotion last season

K

L Huddersfield played their home games here before the John Smith's Stadium

M The scorer of Birmingham's winning goal when they won the League Cup in 2011

GIL MERRICK

Blues' all time appearance maker with 715 appearances including war-time games. Had 22 years at St Andrew's as a goalkeeper and four as manager. First choice for England in his era.

Top class defender who came to St Andrew's as a veteran, making 82 league appearances and later returned to successfully manage the club.

KENNY BURNS

Versatile player who was fearsome everywhere, not just at centre-back. A promotion winner in 1972, this Scotland international played 204 league games, scoring 53 times.

STEVE BRUCE

STAN LYNN

Joint top scorer in 1964/65 despite being a full-back, 'Stan the Wham' scored 30 goals in 148 Blues games, he was part of the League Cup winning team of 1963 who beat his old club Villa in the final.

BILLY HUGHES

Wales international left-back who came to the club in 1934 and was selected for Great Britain in 1947. In a career interrupted by World War Two, Hughes played 110 times for the club.

MIKE HELLAWELL

England international winger who won the League Cup with Blues in 1963. He scored 33 goals in 213 league games for the club and also played cricket for Warwickshire.

TREVOR HOCKEY

STAN LAZARIDIS

Became Blues most capped player by winning 33 caps for Australia while at St Andrew's, left winger Stan had a deceptive change of pace. Made 222 appearances between 1999 and 2006, winning promotion and playing in the 2001 League Cup final.

TERRY HENNESSEY

Wales international, at St Andrew's from 1958. A key player when the Inter-Cities Fairs Cup final was reached and the league Cup won in the early sixties. A great passer, Hennessey played over 200 times for Blues.

BOB LATCHFORD

Birmingham-born centre forward who played in the 1967 FA Youth Cup final and was part of a promotion team five years later. Sold for a record £350,000 in 1974. An England international, his older brother Dave played in goal for Blues.

TREVOR FRANCIS

Trevor Francis was so fast it had to be seen to be believed. Scored 15 in his first 16 games from September 1970. A 1972 promotion winner he totalled 133 in 330 games before being sold in the UK's first £1m deal.

Unmistakeable with his big beard before beards were fashionable, enforcer Hockey made 232 league appearances for Blues mainly in the late sixties. In 1968 he became the youngest player to appear on all 92 league grounds.

23

SPOT THE DIFFERENCE

Can you find the eight differences between these two action shots?

ANSWERS ON PAGE 62

09 Clayton DONALDSON

1

Draw back your foot as if you are going to kick the ball

2

Instead of following through, stop your foot over the ball ...

...and push it back behind your other leg while starting to turn your body.

3

4

Finish turning through 180° and head in the opposite direction.

Your unsuspecting opponent will be left standing wondering what just happened!

5

Johan Cruyff debuted his signature dummy at the 1974 FIFA World Cup. The trick is a brilliant manoeuvre to fool your opponent and change direction.

BIRMINGHAM CITY FOOTBALL CLUB · 1875 ·

ON THE ROAD

Can you figure out where every team in the Championship plays their home games? Fill in the missing words and find all the grounds in the grid!

```
S R F C A R R O W R O A D S L N A L F S J D
E A T O A K W E L L S T A D I U M U K V O F
Y S K W S R I A E K O W O N T F E X B A H G
Q I F M V M D R S J G L D S A W X C T X N I
W S K U I U L I B H E S N J O M S I S D S P
N K G I L I E C F S T B H O U C T T M A M M
A E R D L D M V Y F A O D G Y L A Y U O I U
P L I A A A R G L D C P N Y E N D G I R T I
O A F T P T U J R O A I S G D Y I R D D H D
R D F S A S V D V R F J T R A H U O A N S A
T P I W R I E C K O B T E Y C T M U T A S T
M E N D K K Z M T M D W U G S K E N S L T S
A E P L D S B P A S S O T S F T B D O L A I
N D A R Q J F H N J I M Y Z R U A O R E D L
R C R A V E N C O T T A G E D O E D P N I L
O U K E H D P V J F M S P C I P A R I G U E
A E S S E A L N E W Y O R K S T A D I U M R
D N W X A M U I D A T S X U E N I L O M M I
H I L L S B O R O U G H H Q O H G S G E A T P
```

Team	Ground	Team	Ground	Team	Ground
Aston Villa	Villa Park	Cardiff	Cardiff City Stadium	Nottm Forest	City Ground
Barnsley	Oakwell Stadium	Derby	iPro Stadium	Preston	Deepdale
Birmingham	St Andrews	Fulham	Craven Cottage	QPR	Loftus Road
Blackburn	Ewood Park	Huddersfield	John Smiths Stadium	Reading	Madejski Stadium
Brentford	Griffin Park	Ipswich	Portman Road	Rotherham	AESSEAL New York Stadium
Brighton	Amex Stadium	Leeds	Elland Road	Sheff Wed	Hillsborough
Bristol City	Ashton Gate	Newcastle	St James Park	Wigan	DW Stadium
Burton	Pirelli Stadium	Norwich	Carrow Road	Wolves	Molineux Stadium

ANSWERS ON PAGE 62

Professional footballers at top level can run around 12 kilometres per game...

Quite often, they might have to play two matches within three or four days of each other and over the course of a season, regular players could play in the region of 50 games!

That would be a lot if they were simply running as a long distance runner does. In football though, that running is done with a mixture of short sprints from a standing start and runs of various lengths at differing intensities. On top of this, there is a lot of twisting and turning, often while someone is trying to pull the player back or even kick them. If they can cope with this, there is then the consideration that once the footballer has the ball, they have to use it, either with a telling pass or a shot on goal, while the opposition do all they can to stop them. Added to this is the fact that the thousands of fans watching in the stadium and the millions viewing on TV are only too ready to criticise them if they do not get it right.

To cope with all this, players have to be supremely fit so they have the stamina to last 90 minutes on a regular basis, and have the competitive edge to deal with opponents trying to stop them.

Players also have to be careful to eat and drink the right things, get the right amount of sleep and keep themselves in tip-top shape.

In the summer when players return from a few weeks off, they do a lot of physical training to get themselves ready for the big kick-off. Once a few games have been played and they have, what players call, 'match-fitness', their aim is to maintain that fitness, but not over-do things.

Most players will train for two or three hours most days and do additional work in the gym, as well as perhaps doing pilates or yoga to help look after their bodies. Cycling and swimming can be useful too, but so is knowing when to simply rest, because the Championship season is a long and gruelling campaign.

PRE-SEASON TRAINING

07 Robert TESCHE

Can you work out in which season each of these photos was taken?

There's a clue to help you with each one!

spot the season

A

Frank Worthington was top scorer with 18 goals this season

B

Birmingham beat Arsenal 2-1 to become League Cup winners this season

C

Ken Leek scored in the first leg of the League Cup final, which Blues went on to win this season

D

This was the first season Birmingham played under legend Trevor Francis

E

Blues were Second Division Champions this season

DANGER MEN

ASTON VILLA
ROSS McCORMACK

One of the costliest strikers in the Championship, Scotland international McCormack cost Fulham £11m in 2014 with the Cottagers making a profit of £1m when Villa bought the Glasgow born hot-shot at the start of this season. The 30-year-old has scored over 150 goals in his career and is a man who makes many more.

BARNSLEY
TOM BRADSHAW

Having scored 20 goals in each of the last two seasons Bradshaw was disappointed to lose to Barnsley in last season's League One Play-offs for Walsall - but then signed for the Tykes. Having scored a League Cup hat-trick against Championship side Forest last season, the Wales international got his first goal in this season's Championship in a South Yorkshire derby against Rotherham at the end of August.

BIRMINGHAM CITY
CLAYTON DONALDSON

Jamaican international Donaldson is a great spearhead for Blues. Good in the air, determined and mobile he has scored over 40 goals for three different clubs and could equal that achievement with a good season for Birmingham for whom he has bagged 27 in the past two seasons.

BLACKBURN ROVERS
DANNY GRAHAM

A well-travelled target man, Danny Graham impressed on loan for Rovers last season before signing for them in the summer. With well over 100 goals in his career, Graham's best haul was 27 with Watford in 2010/11 - 24 of those were in the Championship in what was his last full season spent at this level.

BRENTFORD
SCOTT HOGAN

Hogan could be a hero for the Bees this season and be their secret weapon. Having played for six non-league clubs he was given a chance by Rochdale who he had played for at Academy level. Hogan quickly made up for lost time, a debut goal being Sky TV's 'Goal of the Day'. It was the first of 19 he got that season as he fired Rochdale to promotion, was voted Player of the Year and into the PFA League 2 team. Badly injured soon after a move to Brentford, he returned with seven goals in seven games late last season.

BRIGHTON & HOVE ALBION
TOMER HEMED

The 29-year-old Israel international is a big part of Brighton's promotion hopes. Having played in Spain as well as his home country, Hemed scored 16 goals in 40 games in his first season in English football last season and Chris Hughton will look to bring the best out of him once again this time round.

BRISTOL CITY
TAMMY ABRAHAM

With 74 goals in 98 games for Chelsea at youth level the question is can England U20 speed merchant Abraham do it at first team level? Given a Chelsea debut v Liverpool last season, he took 15 minutes of his debut on loan to Bristol City to find the net and did so four more times in his next five games. If Tammy keeps it up he could be this season's 'Rockin' Robin'.

BURTON ALBION
CHRIS O'GRADY

O'Grady has had so many loans he might think he's a high street bank, his current stint with Burton being his tenth. On loan from Brighton, Chris started this season three goals short of a century. Not always prolific, he can be - netting 15 in 2013/14 - but he's always a handful and is key to Burton doing well this season following last year's promotion.

CARDIFF CITY
RICKIE LAMBERT

Approaching 250 career goals - over 100 of them for one club (Southampton) - Rickie Lambert is a lethal finisher. The sheer number of his goals earned him an England debut in 2013 and he scored with his first touch, heading home against Scotland. Now 32, Lambert isn't the quickest, but his game has never been based on pace.

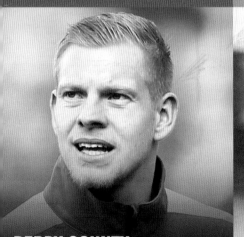

DERBY COUNTY
MATEJ VYDRA

The Rams paid a reported £8m to snap up the 24-year-old Czech Republic hitman who was the Championship Player of the Year in 2013 after netting 20 goals in 41 games for Watford. A nippy goal-poacher Vydra played in his home country as well as Italy and Belgium before coming into English football where he has also played for WBA and Reading.

FULHAM
CHRIS MARTIN

Chris Martin might feel destiny would bring him to Fulham who he joined on a season-long loan from Derby just as the transfer window closed. Having played for England at U19 level he decided to play for Scotland and made his international debut in 2014 against Nigeria...at Fulham's Craven Cottage! Great in the air, Martin is one of the best strikers in the league.

HUDDERSFIELD TOWN
NAHKI WELLS

Having hit 17 goals last season, Wells will hope to maintain that level of consistency for the Terriers. Nahki came to the fore at nearby Bradford City for whom he played in the League Cup final in 2013 after scoring in the semi-final against Aston Villa. Pacey, persistent and with the ability to finish, Wells is always a tough customer.

Watch out for these dangermen when Blues meet their Championship rivals...

IPSWICH TOWN
BRETT PITMAN

A consistent goal-scorer who notched 11 goals for the Tractor Boys last season and 14 the year before as part of Bournemouth's title-winning team. Following Ipswich's sale of Daryl Murphy to Newcastle at the start of the season, the club's need for Pitman to be among the goals will be even more important this time round.

LEEDS UNITED
CHRIS WOOD

Twice a promotion winner to the Premier League, Leeds will hope Wood can complete a notable hat-trick at Elland Road. A New Zealand international who played at the World Cup finals in 2010, Chris won promotion to the Championship with Brighton and into the top flight with both West Brom and Leicester.

NEWCASTLE UNITED
DWIGHT GAYLE

Lift off for the man whose first club was Stansted came when Newcastle United paid £10m to bring the Londoner from Crystal Palace. Gayle's first ever Premier League goal came against Newcastle in his Palace days and he made a good start at firing the Magpies back towards the top flight with four goals in his first four games for Rafa Benitez's side.

NORWICH CITY
SERGI CANOS

A former Barcelona youth player, Sergi played once for Liverpool before spending last season on loan to Brentford where he scored seven and made five goals as a winger. Still a teenager the Spain U19 international cost the Canaries £2.5m in the summer to bring him from Anfield and he could well be a potent weapon whenever he is on the ball for City.

NOTTINGHAM FOREST
BRITT ASSOMBALONGA

23 goals in 43 games for Peterborough in 2013/14 signalled Assombalonga's goal threat, Posh having already recognised that when making the Watford Academy product their record signing. A bad injury cost Britt 14 months of his career having also broken Forest's transfer record but with 19 goals in his first 36 games he remains one of the hottest properties in the Championship.

PRESTON NORTH END
DANIEL JOHNSON

Given a new contract early this season, Johnson is Preston's midfield creator and offers a goal threat coming in from the left. Having been schooled in the youth systems at Palace and Villa the Jamaican came to Preston in January 2015, helped North End to promotion and is at the heart of much of their best attacking play.

QUEENS PARK RANGERS
TJARONN CHERY

Hoops' Player of the Year last season, Tjaronn scored three goals in the first four games of this season, his first campaign in English football. Now 28, Chery was called into an international squad for Holland in May 2015 after scoring 15 times in his last season with Groningen.

READING
YANN KERMORGANT

The aerial ability of the veteran French striker can be a key asset for Jaap Stam's side. Kermorgant helped Bournemouth to the Championship title in 2015 when he scored 17 goals in all competitions and was nominated for the Championship goal of the season for one of his trademark bicycle kicks.

ROTHERHAM UNITED
DANNY WARD

Rotherham will fight hard to stay up this year with Danny Ward a key man for the Millers. He scored on the opening day of the season against Wolves and soon followed that up with a vital winner against Brentford. On his day he can be lethal, as he showed with a Championship hat-trick away to Watford in May 2014 in his Huddersfield days. 25 just before Christmas, Ward's form is likely to be key to Rotherham's progress.

SHEFFIELD WEDNESDAY
STEVEN FLETCHER

Scotland international striker Fletcher spent the latter part of last season in France with Marseille - making his debut against PSG when he came on for Michy Batshuayi who Chelsea have since paid mega-money for. One of the best headers of the ball in the game, the former Hibs, Burnley, Wolves and Sunderland man can be deadly on any day of the week.

WIGAN ATHLETIC
WILL GRIGG

The song 'Will Grigg's on fire' reached the iTunes top 10 last season as the Northern Ireland international fired in 28 goals on top of the 22 he'd struck the season before. Showing no signs that his form had been dampened the 25-year-old began with a bang this term, scoring four times in his first five games. If he's heading for your defence dial 999 in case of emergency.

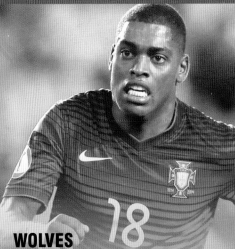

WOLVES
IVAN CAVALEIRO

As a former goalie, Wolves boss Walter Zenga knows a dangerman when he sees one and broke Wanderers' club record to bring in Portugal international Cavaleiro for a reported £7m. The 23-year-old can play on the wing or up front and has played Champions League football for Benfica and Monaco. As an U21 international he hit a hat-trick on his debut against Switzerland in 2013.

19 Jacques MAGHOMA

Can you figure out the identity of these Blues stars?

ANSWERS ON PAGE 62

A

B

E

Who are yer?

888 sport

adidas

Che Adams

After a summer of rumours, Gary Rowett was finally able to bag his man on a permanent transfer.

Adams, who is 20, is seen as a perfect signing with Blues able to nurture the striker's talent ahead of his prime years.

Adams started his career at Coventry City's youth academy before spells in non-league with Oadby Town and Ilkeston. Scouts flocked to see his star performances and Sheffield United secured his signing in 2014.

The pacey frontman showed his promise in front of the Sky cameras as he netted two late goals in Sheffield United's League Cup semi-final home defeat to Tottenham Hotspur. Adams' skills were clear to see and after 47 appearances, scoring 11 goals, Blues were able to beat off the opposition to secure his signature.

STAR SIGNING

1

2

3

4

5

6

7

8

9

SKILLS: Rainbow Kick

1
Start off with your feet on either side of the ball

2
Use one foot to roll the ball up your other leg

3
Make sure to roll the ball hard enough to give it some air

4
When the ball is in the air strike it with your heel

5
...and flick it over your head!

Brazilian star striker, Neymar, is well known for his use of the rainbow kick on the pitch and regularly fools his opposition. The trick is an impressive show of skill which takes practise, practise practise!

TIP: Lean forward as you're doing the trick, this helps create space between you and the ball so you can strike it more easily.

08 Stephen GLEESON

43

Here is the second half of our Championship A-Z.

The answer to each clue begins with the corresponding letter of the alphabet.

A-Z OF THE

N QPR manager Jimmy Floyd Hasselbaink played for this national team

O He scored the winning goal when Ipswich won the FA Cup in 1978

One of Brentford's main rivals

P Fulham captain and former England international

Q

R Aston Villa's number four defender

S The team Norwich beat in the final of the League Cup in 1985

CHAMPIONSHIP

See how much you really know!

T — arnsley's nickname

U — The animal on Bristol City's crest

V — Nottingham Forest's Dutch 'keeper

W — Sheffield Wednesday's goalie

X — Newcastle manager, Rafa Benitez, bought and sold this Spanish midfielder while at Liverpool

Y — Young Rotherham forward

Z — Danish striker who signed for Cardiff this summer

CLUB OR COUNTRY?

Can you work out which team each set of clues is pointing to... they could be Premier League, Championship or international.

1. Hull City

2. Newcastle

3. Spain

4. Austria

5. Wigan

6. Tottenham

7. Iceland

8. Arsenal

9. Wolves

46

ANSWERS ON PAGE 62

11 David COTTERILL

47

HAT-TRICK

There's very little to put a smile on a striker's face more than scoring a hat-trick in a winning performance.

Take a look back at three special Blues trebles...

MIKAEL FORSSELL
V SPURS (2008)

The Finnish striker scored his first club level hat-trick in Blues' 4-1 win over Tottenham Hotspur in 2008.

Spurs, who had beaten Chelsea to lift the Carling Cup the previous week, were no match for Forssell's excellent performance. The striker's first goal came after six minutes with a headed effort and his late double with both feet earned him the man of the match accolade with a perfect hat-trick.

CLAYTON DONALDSON
V BRISTOL CITY (2015)

Blues' excellent start to the season was showcased in their 4-2 win over Bristol City. Donaldson, who netted a first-half hat-trick, made it 2-0 before Jonathan Kodjia clawed one back.

Blues immediately won a penalty and after a short conversation, regular taker Paul Caddis allowed the striker to net from the spot. Donaldson showed his emotions after the finish, as he became a father for the first time, earlier that week.

HEROES

GARY McSHEFFREY
V PRESTON (2006)

Blues' return to the Premier League remained on course as McSheffrey netted an excellent hat-trick. The winger, who'd signed from boyhood Coventry City that summer, netted two first-half goals against Preston North End.

The away side held their own in the second-half, but Blues capped off a good performance in the 89th minute. McSheffrey was fouled by Sean St. Ledger in the penalty area and he secured the match ball by finishing past Carlo Nash.

551 TOTAL APPEARANCES

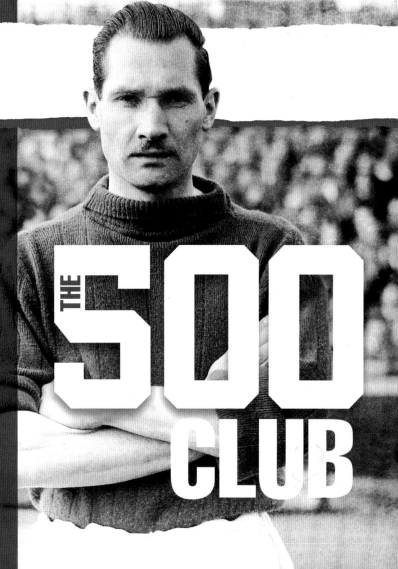

GIL MERRICK

Born in Sparkhill, Merrick is the quintessential Bluenose. After signing professional terms in 1939, he remained at the Club until 1960 amassing a total of 551 appearances.

Considered one of the best goalkeepers in the UK during his era, Merrick earned 23 caps for England with his final three fixtures during the 1954 World Cup.

Merrick took over the managerial reigns from Pat Beasley and led Blues to their first major trophy, the League Cup, in 1963, beating Aston Villa 3-1 on aggregate.

A year before Merrick's death in 2010, the Club honoured the 'keeper by renaming the Railway End Stand to the Gil Merrick Stand. Later that year, Merrick was chosen by public vote as Birmingham City's representative on the Birmingham Walk of Stars as well as he first inductee to the Birmingham City FC Hall of Fame.

THE 500 CLUB

FRANK WOMACK

Originally starting at Rawmarsh Albion near Rotherham, full-back Frank Womack joined Blues in 1908 as a full-back. Womack, who skippered Blues for 17 consecutive seasons in a 20-year association became one of the best Midland full-back's of his era, which included West Brom's England international Jesse Pennington.

After making 515 appearances and helping Blues to the Second Division title in 1921, Womack became the first player-manager to be appointed in the Birmingham League in 1928.

Managerial spells at Torquay United, Grimsby Town, Leicester City, Notts County and Oldham Athletic followed before he left in the game in 1951. Womack sadly passed in 1968, aged 80, but many of his records are still intact. Womack still holds the league record for most games (511) by an outfield player without scoring a goal and at 39 years, 207 days old, he is the second oldest player ever to appear for Blues in a first-class match.

515 TOTAL APPEARANCES

BIRMINGHAM CITY FOOTBALL CLUB · 1875 ·

FANTASTIC

Can you find them all?

SKILLS: Maradona Spin

1 Start off by simply dribbling the ball

2 While moving in a forward motion, tap the ball with your leading foot...

3 ...and start turning your body in the opposite direction

4

5 As you're spinning, pull the ball back with your other foot while continuing to turn

6 Then keep moving forward!

Argentinian maestro, Maradona, is very well known for this move. It is brilliant for overcoming opponents and getting yourself into space, as while you are spinning you are putting your back to the defender and shielding the ball.

38 Jack STORER

A

Ken Charlery celebrates
scoring on his debut

Can you work out in which season each of these photos was taken?

There's a clue to help you with each one!

B

This was Maik Taylor's second
season after signing a permanent
contract with Birmingham City

C

Manager Steve Bruce arrived this season

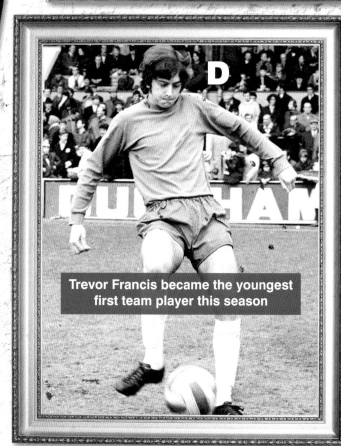

D

Trevor Francis became the youngest
first team player this season

E

Goalkeeper Gil Merrick was top
appearance maker this season
with a total of 48 games

spot the
Season

Viv Solomon-Otabor

Viv Solomon-Otabor's quick progression to the First Team has made plenty of scouts take note.

Solomon-Otabor, who was born in London joined Crystal Palace's academy before taking up a scholarship with the Club in 2012. Under the tutelage of Richard Beale, the pacey winger signed his first professional deal in 2014 and he became a key part of the Development Squad that won the Birmingham Senior Cup.

Solomon-Otabor's talent was noted by manager Gary Rowett and he was given a squad number ahead of Blues' second-round League Cup tie against Gillingham at home last season. The winger made his debut in the 2-0 win after 77 minutes, whilst his league debut followed a month later.

His performances were impressive and he made his biggest impact at Craven Cottage when his excellent solo effort from deep inside Blues' half topped off Blues' 5-2 win at Fulham. With the departure of Demarai Gray to Leicester, Solomon -Otabor signed a new three-and-a-half-year contact and he finished the campaign with 23 appearances and one goal.

During the close season, he earned the Club's Young Player of the Season award for 2015/16 and was selected for Nigeria's Olympic football team.

WonderKID

FIVE GAMES TO LOOK FOR IN THE SECOND HALF OF THE SEASON

The second half of the 2016/17 season certainly looks to be an exciting affair for all at St Andrew's. We take a look at five key fixtures scheduled for the latter stages of the current campaign.

MONDAY 2 JANUARY · ST ANDREW'S

BRENTFORD

Similar to last season, Blues start the calendar year by hosting Brentford at St Andrew's. Blues boss Gary Rowett will be hoping his side replicate last years excellent performance that continued a good run of form.

Jacques Maghoma's solo effort gave Blues a deserved lead, but Brentford equalised after 77 minutes. With both sides pushing for the win, Maikel Kieftenbeld ran from deep and finished an excellent counter attacking move to send a boisterous St Andrew's into raptures.

SATURDAY 25 FEBRUARY MOLINEUX STADIUM

WOLVES

Birmingham City head to Wolverhampton Wanderers for a passionate derby that always provides drama. Blues have enjoyed plenty of monumental wins at Molineux!

Last season, Blues were unlucky to not take three points against Kenny Jackett's side, while this season Gary Rowett will be looking to avenge Wolves' 3-1 win over Blues at St Andrew's in August.

SATURDAY 8 APRIL · ST ANDREW'S

DERBY COUNTY

Promotion hopefuls Derby County will head to St Andrew's with both sides hoping to be firmly in the promotion race.

The Rams, who recruited heavily over the summer, will have happy memories of St Andrew's after picking up four points from their past two visits. However, it's not all smiles in the East Midlands. Blues have provided plenty of drama after coming back from 2-0 down in the 2014/15 season and beating them 3-0 at the iPro Stadium last season.

SUNDAY 23 APRIL · VILLA PARK

ASTON VILLA

This fixture needs no introduction as there'll be plenty of bragging rights in the passionate Second City derby.

Blues' last league trip to Villa Park outside the top flight came in 1987 when they won 2-0. Blues will be looking to mirror that win and avenge Aston Villa's 1-0 victory in last season's Capital One Cup.

SUNDAY 7 MAY · ASHTON GATE STADIUM

BRISTOL CITY

Blues end their 2016/17 campaign at the rebuilt Ashton Gate Stadium. The Robins, who finished 18th last season, will be hoping to have made significant progress under new ownership, whilst Blues will be looking to travel to the West Country in partisan spirits like last season.

Last year's trip to Bristol ended in a tight 0-0 draw, but the fixture will be fondly remembered as the permanent return of Italian midfielder Diego Fabbrini.

January 2017

Mon	02	Brentford	H	3.00pm
Sat	14	Nottingham Forest	H	3.00pm
Sat	21	Blackburn	A	3.00pm
Sat	28	Norwich City	A	3.00pm
Tue	31	Reading	H	7.45pm

February 2017

Sat	04	Fulham	H	3.00pm
Sat	11	Sheff Wed	A	3.00pm
Tue	14	Preston North End	A	7.45pm
Sat	18	QPR	H	3.00pm
Sat	25	Wolves	A	3.00pm

March 2017

Sat	04	Leeds	H	3.00pm
Tue	07	Wigan	H	7.45pm
Sat	11	Cardiff	A	3.00pm
Sat	18	Newcastle	H	3.00pm

April 2017

Sat	01	Ipswich	A	3.00pm
Tue	04	Brighton	A	7.45pm
Sat	08	Derby	H	3.00pm
Fri	14	Rotherham	A	3.00pm
Mon	17	Burton Albion	H	3.00pm
Sun	23	Aston Villa	A	12 noon
Sat	29	Huddersfield	H	3.00pm

May 2017

Sun	07	Bristol City	A	12 noon

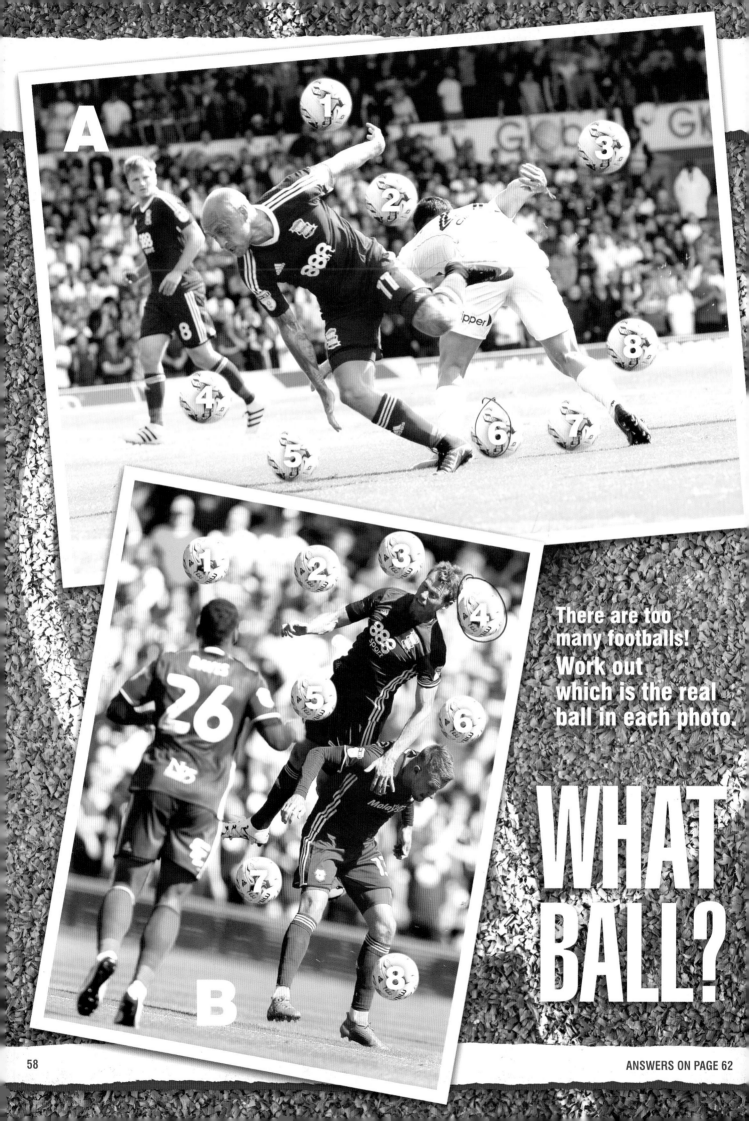

There are too
many footballs!
Work out
which is the real
ball in each photo.

WHAT BALL?

ANSWERS ON PAGE 62

28 Michael MORRISON

PREMIER LEAGUE

PREDICTION FOR CHAMPIONSHIP WINNERS:

YOUR PREDICTION: blues

PREDICTION FOR ALSO PROMOTED TO THE PREMIER LEAGUE:

YOUR PREDICTION: necastel

PREDICTION FOR PREMIER LEAGUE WINNERS:

YOUR PREDICTION: chealse

PREDICTION FOR PREMIER LEAGUE RUNNERS-UP:

YOUR PREDICTION: manchester unted

THE CHAMPIONSHIP

PREDICTIONS

THE FA CUP

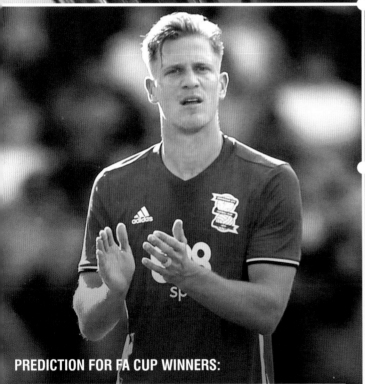

PREDICTION FOR FA CUP WINNERS:

YOUR PREDICTION: arsenal

PREDICTION FOR FA CUP FINALISTS:

YOUR PREDICTION: chelsea

PREDICTION FOR LEAGUE CUP WINNERS:

YOUR PREDICTION: liverpool

PREDICTION FOR LEAGUE CUP FINALISTS:

YOUR PREDICTION: man u

THE LEAGUE CUP

ANSWERS

PAGE 19 · SPOT THE SEASON

a. 1971/72, b. 1979/80, c. 1905/06, d. 2012/13, e. 1990/91.

PAGE 20 · A-Z OF THE CHAMPIONSHIP

a. Aston Villa, b. Bees, c. Nigel Clough, d. Deepdale,
e. Dave Edwards, f. Falmer Stadium, g. Chris Gunter,
h. Grant Hanley, i. iPro Stadium, j. Jussi Jaaskelainen,
k. Kappa, l. Leeds Road, m. Obafemi Martins.

PAGE 24 · SPOT THE DIFFERENCE

PAGE 27 · ON THE ROAD

Aston Villa - Villa Park, Barnsley - Oakwell Stadium,
Birmingham - St Andrew's, Blackburn - Ewood Park,
Brentford - Griffin Park, Brighton - AMEX Stadium,
Bristol City - Ashton Gate, Burton - Pirelli Stadium,
Cardiff - Cardiff City Stadium, Derby - iPro Stadium,
Fulham - Craven Cottage, Huddersfield - John Smith's Stadium,
Ipswich - Portman Road, Leeds - Elland Road,
Newcastle - St James' Park, Norwich - Carrow Road,
Nottm Forest - City Ground, Preston - Deepdale,
QPR - Loftus Road, Reading - Madejski Stadium,
Rotherham - AESSEAL New York Stadium, Sheff Wed - Hillsborough,
Wigan - DW Stadium, Wolves - Molineux Stadium.

PAGE 31 · SPOT THE SEASON

a. 1980/81, b. 2010/11, c. 1962/63, d. 1996/97, e. 1954/55.

PAGE 38 · WHO ARE YER?

a. Diego Fabbrini, b. Clayton Donaldson, c. Adam Legzdins,
d. Jacques Maghoma, e. David Cotterill, f. Robert Tesche,
g. Jonathan Grounds.

PAGE 41 · FACE OFF

1. Ryan Shotton, 2. Reece Brown, 3. Jacques Maghoma,
4. Tomasz Kuszczak, 5. Clayton Donaldson, 6. Maikel Kieftenbeld,
7. Jack Storer, 8. Jonathan Spector, 9. Adam Legzdins.

PAGE 44 · A-Z OF THE CHAMPIONSHIP

n. the Netherlands, o. Roger Osborne, p. Scott Parker, q. QPR,
r. Micah Richards, s. Sunderland, t. the Tykes, u. Unicorn,
v. Dorus de Vries, w. Keiren Westwood, x. Xabi Alonso,
y. Jerry Yates, z. Kenneth Zohore

PAGE 46 · CLUB OR COUNTRY?

1. Hull City, 2. Newcastle United, 3. Spain, 4. Austria,
5. Wigan Athletic, 6. Tottenham Hotspur, 7. Iceland,
8. Arsenal, 9. Wolverhampton Wanderers.

PAGE 50 · FANTASTIC

Greg Rutherford, Andy Murray, Jessica Ennis-Hill,
Bradley Wiggins and Nicola Adams.

PAGE 54 · SPOT THE SEASON

a. 1995/96, b. 2004/05, c. 2001/02,
d. 1970/71, e. 1950/51.

PAGE 58 · WHAT BALL?

Picture A - Ball 6,
Picture B - Ball 4.